AAT Foundation Certificate in Accounting
Level 2
Bookkeeping Controls

Second edition 2017

ISBN 9781 5097 1238 0

British Library Cataloguing-in-Publication Data

A catalogue record for this book is available from the British Library

Published by

BPP Learning Media Ltd
BPP House, Aldine Place
142-144 Uxbridge Road
London W12 8AA

www.bpp.com/learningmedia

Printed in the United Kingdom

Your learning materials, published by BPP Learning Media Ltd, are printed on paper obtained from traceable sustainable sources.

Welcome to BPP Learning Media's AAT **Passcards for Bookkeeping Controls**.

- They **save you time**. Important topics are summarised for you.

- They incorporate **diagrams** to kick start your memory.

- They follow the overall **structure** of the BPP Course Book but BPP's AAT **Passcards** are not just a condensed book. Each card has been separately designed for clear presentation. Topics are self contained and can be grasped visually.

- AAT **Passcards** are **just the right size** for pockets and bags.

- AAT **Passcards focus on the assessment** you will be facing.

- AAT **Passcards focus on the essential points** you need to know in the workplace, or when completing your assessment.

Run through the complete set of **Passcards** as often as you can during your final revision period. The day before the assessment, try to go through the **Passcards** again! You will then be well on your way to completing the assessment successfully.

Good luck!

		Page

The BPP **Question Bank** contains activities and assessments that provide invaluable practice in the skills you need to complete this unit successfully.

1: Payment methods

Cash flow is crucial to a business. In this chapter, the different payment methods available are considered together with the effect they have on the bank balance.

Payment methods which have an immediate effect on the bank account

Payment method	Use	Effect on bank
Cash (withdrawn from the bank)	Small value transactions	Immediate
Debit card	Online, telephone, in person payment transactions	Automatic and immediate
Bank draft	For guaranteed payments, such as vehicle purchases or overseas payments	Immediate on the payer (only affects the payee once they have banked the draft)
Standing order	Regular, same value payments. Set up by the payee (eg rent)	Immediate, regular
Direct debit	Regular payments which the receiver can vary if required (eg utility bills)	Immediate, regular

Payment method	Use	Effect on bank
BACS direct credit	Electronic bank payment initiated by the payer (eg salaries, paying suppliers on credit)	Immediate, regular payments
CHAPS	Non-cancellable funds transfer used for large purchases, such as property purchases	Immediate, regular payments
Faster payments	Same day small/medium payments (suppliers)	Immediate (usually within two hours)

Payment methods which have no effect on the bank account

Payment method	Use	Effect on bank
Cash (from the till)	Small value transactions	Cash from till has no effect until banked

Payment methods which have a delayed effect on the bank account

Payment method	Use	Effect on bank
Cheque	To pay for purchases made on credit	Delayed until banked by the payee (three working days)
Credit card	Online, telephone, in person payment transactions	No effect on the bank until the credit card statement is settled

Assessment Focus Point: Questions may require you to select the appropriate payment method based on the detail provided in the question scenario. You also need to understand the impact that different payment methods have on the bank account.

2: Bank reconciliations

In theory the entries on the business's bank statement should be exactly the same as those in the business's cash book. In practice, the entries and the balances will differ.

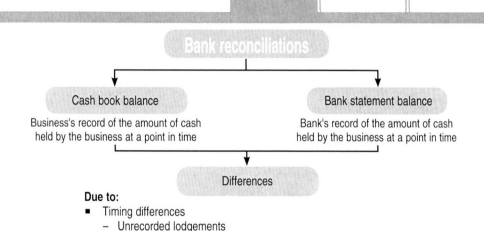

The following tabs appear at the top of the figure: **Purpose** | Proforma | Example

Bank reconciliations

Cash book balance

Business's record of the amount of cash held by the business at a point in time

Bank statement balance

Bank's record of the amount of cash held by the business at a point in time

Differences

Due to:
- Timing differences
  - Unrecorded lodgements
  - Outstanding cheques
- Cash book needs to be updated
  - Standing orders, direct debits
  - Bank charges, interest (received or charged)
  - BACS direct credits, payments to staff, monies received electronically

Bank reconciliation process

1. Compare the following
   - DEBIT side of the cashbook = PAID IN on the bank statement
   - CREDIT side of the cashbook = PAID OUT on the bank statement
2. Unmatched items on the bank statement are OMISSIONS and must be entered in the cashbook
3. Unmatched items on the cashbook are TIMING DIFFERENCES

Bank reconciliation statement	£
Balance per bank statement	X
Add:	
Total to add	X
Less:	
Total to subtract	X
Balance as per cash book	X

Cashbook

Details	Bank £	Details	Bank £
Balance b/f	X	Bank charges	X
Bank interest	X	Standing orders	X
Counter credit	X	Direct debits	X
		Cheques	X

Example

The following is Jack's cash book.

Date 20XX	Details	Bank £	Date 20XX	Details	Bank £
1 March	Balance b/f	150	8 March	Spratt	30
6 March	Cash	75	16 March	Tuffet	15
13 March	Jill	17	28 March	Spider	29
31 March	Humpty	39	31 March	Balance c/d	207
		281			281

On 31 March 20XX Jack received the following bank statement.

Date 20XX	Details	Paid out £	Paid in £	Balance £
1 March	Balance			150C
6 March	Cash		75	225C
10 March	Spratt	30		195C
13 March	Jill		17	212C
15 March	Credit transfer – Bill		16	228C
18 March	Tuffet	15		213C
31 March	Charges	10		203C

Bring the cash book up-to-date, state the new balance at 31 March 20XX and prepare a statement to reconcile the difference between the new up-to-date balance in the cash book and the balance on the bank statement on 31 March 20XX.

Date 20XX	Details	Bank £	Date 20XX	Details	Bank £
1 March	Balance b/f	150	8 March	Spratt	30
6 March	Cash	75	16 March	Tuffet	15
13 March	Jill	17	28 March	Spider	29
31 March	Humpty	39	**31 March**	**Bank charges**	**10**
15 March	**Credit: Bill**	**16**	**31 March**	**Balance c/d**	**213**
		297			297
1 April	**Balance b/d**	213			

Bank reconciliation statement at 31 Mar 20XX	£
Balance per bank statement	203
Add:	
Humpty	39
Total to add	39
Less:	
Spider	29
Total to subtract	29
Balance as per cash book	213

3: Introduction to control accounts

In this chapter we look at the function of control accounts and how they are prepared from the books of prime entry.

What are control accounts?

A control account is a **total** account.

Control accounts contain summarised totals of all the individual transactions.

- The sales ledger control account records totals of credit customer transactions.

- The purchases ledger control account records totals of credit suppliers.

- Subsidiary ledgers are prepared so that the business can see the amount owed from the credit customers or to credit suppliers. The separate accounts list the details behind the transactions (invoice, date, payments etc).

Business transactions are recorded in the books of prime entry. For example, sales invoices are recorded in the sales day book.

Three important control accounts are
- sales ledger control account
- purchases ledger control account
- VAT control account

This minimises the transactions posted to the general ledger (less room for error). The accuracy of the general ledger and subsidiary ledgers can be checked by reconciling their balances.

The diagram overleaf illustrates how credit sales are introduced into the double entry system.

The invoices in the sales day book are totalled periodically and the total amount is posted in the general ledger as follows.

DEBIT   Sales ledger control account

CREDIT   Sales account(s)
CREDIT   VAT account

Similarly, the total of cash receipts from credit customers is posted from the cash book to the credit of the sales ledger control account.

In the same way, the purchases ledger control account is credited with the total purchase invoices logged in the purchases day book and debited with the total of payments to credit suppliers.

DEBIT   Purchases
DEBIT   VAT account

CREDIT   Purchases ledger control account

Overview of sales invoice processing

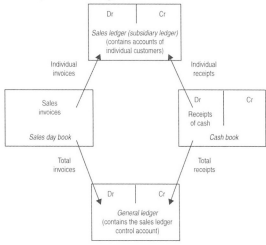

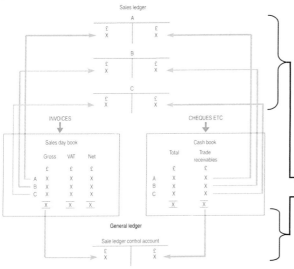

Control account reconciliation

The control account should be balanced regularly. The balance should be the same as the sum of the balances on the sales or purchases ledger (ie individual customers'/suppliers' accounts).

This is the step by step approach for a sales ledger control account, but the same procedure is followed for a purchases ledger control account reconciliation.

Step 1 Balance off each of the individual sales ledger accounts

➤Step 2 Add up all of the individual sales ledger balances

➤Step 3 Balance off the sales ledger control account in the general ledger

The total at Step 2 should equal the total at Step 3

VAT control account

The VAT control account works in a similar way to the sales and purchases ledger control accounts except that there is not an underlying subsidiary ledger. At its simplest:

- VAT amounts on sales and purchase invoices are recorded in the day books and then totals are posted to the VAT control account.

- Payments to HM Revenue & Customs (HMRC) of VAT owed is recorded in the credit side of the Cash Book and debited to the VAT control account.

- Receipts of VAT refunds from HMRC are recorded in the debit side of the Cash Book and credited to the VAT control account.

- The balance on the VAT control account shows how much is due to HMRC (credit balance) or repayable by HMRC (debit balance).

Details	Amount £	Details	Amount £
Sales returns	500	Balance b/d	3,000
Purchases	4,000	Sales	5,000
Discounts allowed	200	Cash sales	300
Bank	2,800	Purchases returns	600
Balance c/d	1,500	Discounts received	100
	9,000		9,000
		Balance b/d	1,500

Money owed to HMRC at the start of the period ← (pointing to Balance b/d 3,000)

The entries in respect of VAT, sales ledger and purchases ledger control accounts are considered in more detail in the next chapter.

Money owed to HMRC at the end of the period (c/d), and brought forward (b/f) at the start of the next period → (pointing to Balance c/d 1,500 and Balance b/d 1,500)

Assessment Focus Point: You may be asked to prepare the journals for, or complete a VAT control account. It is important to understand the debits and credits in this control account.

3: Introduction to control accounts

4: Preparing and reconciling control accounts

Control accounts help highlight human error. They also allow for last minute adjustments for items such as irrecoverable debts.

Sales ledger control account (SLCA)

Total owed to the business at the start of the period by credit customers → Balance b/f

Posted from the total column in the sales day book → Credit sales

Posted from the total column in the sales returns day book → Credit sales returns

Trade receivables column in the cash book (debit side) → Payments from customers

Posted from the memorandum column in the cash book (debit side) → Discounts allowed

Double entry for this is:
DEBIT Irrecoverable debts expense (net)
DEBIT VAT control (only if VAT was charged on the original entry)
CREDIT SLCA (gross)
→ Irrecoverable debts written off

The balancing figure at the end of the period = total owed by credit customers at end of period → Balance c/d

Balance b/d ←

Sales ledger control account (SLCA)			
	£		£
Balance b/f	X	Credit sales returns	X
Credit sales	X	Payments from customers	X
		Discounts allowed	X
		Irrecoverable debts written off	X
		Balance c/d	X
	X		X
Balance b/d	X		

Posted from the total column in the purchases returns day book →

Trade payables column in the cash book (credit side) →

Posted from the memorandum column on the cash book (credit side) →

The amount owed at the end of the period. This is the period end PLCA balance to reconcile with the individual purchases ledger balances.

Purchases ledger control account			
	£		£
Credit purchases returns	X	Balance b/f	X
Payments to suppliers	X	Credit purchases	X
Discounts received	X		
Balance c/d	X		
	X		X
		Balance b/d	X

← Total owed by the business at the start of the period to credit suppliers

← Posted from the total column on the purchases day book

Assessment Focus Point: You could be asked to prepare a table and calculate the balances carried down/brought down.

4: Preparing and reconciling control accounts

Learn the step by step approach below. This is for a sales ledger control account, but the same procedure is followed for a purchases ledger control account reconciliation.

1. Balance the accounts in the sales ledger and review for errors.

2. Calculate the total of balances extracted from the sales ledger and calculate a total of all the balances.

3. Balance the sales ledger control account and review for errors.

4. Identify reasons for discrepancies between the control accounts and the individual ledgers.

Possible reasons for credit balances on sales ledger accounts, or for debit balances on purchases ledger accounts:

- Overpayment of amount owed
- Return of goods
- Payment in advance
- Posting errors

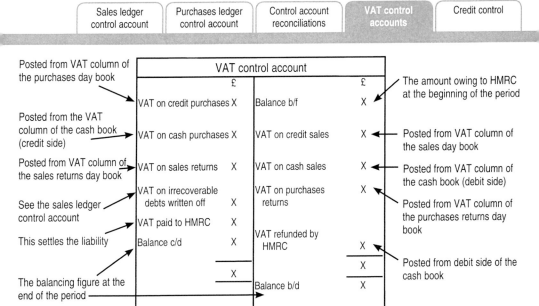

VAT control account

Posted from VAT column of the purchases day book → VAT on credit purchases X

Balance b/f X ← The amount owing to HMRC at the beginning of the period

Posted from the VAT column of the cash book (credit side) → VAT on cash purchases X

VAT on credit sales X ← Posted from VAT column of the sales day book

Posted from VAT column of the sales returns day book → VAT on sales returns X

VAT on cash sales X ← Posted from VAT column of the cash book (debit side)

See the sales ledger control account → VAT on irrecoverable debts written off X

VAT on purchases returns X ← Posted from VAT column of the purchases returns day book

This settles the liability → VAT paid to HMRC X

Balance c/d X

VAT refunded by HMRC X ← Posted from debit side of the cash book

X

X

The balancing figure at the end of the period → Balance b/d X

- Ensures receivables are paid on time, any late payers are followed up promptly
- A business uses the subsidiary sales ledger accounts to identify overdue debts
- An aged receivables analysis allows the credit controller to see how long debts have been outstanding
- If a business believes a debt is definitely irrecoverable, it is no longer an asset of the business and should be written off

DEBIT Irrecoverable debt expense
DEBIT VAT control account

CREDIT Sales ledger control account

> Assessment Focus Point: You are likely to be required to write off an irrecoverable debt

5: The journal

The journal is the final book of prime entry to be considered. We cover the format and uses of a journal entry.

Book of prime entry

The journal is a book of prime entry recording transactions that do not appear in any other book of prime entry.

These can then be posted to the general ledger and include:

- Writing off an irrecoverable debt
- Posting opening balances
- Payroll transactions

Journal number		0001	Paid in £
Date	Reference	16 Mar 20XX	
Authorised by		JH Smith	
Account		A Khan	
Account name		Debit £	Credit £
Irrecoverable debts expense	GL020	100.00	
VAT control	GL135	20.00	
Sales ledger control	GL106		120.00
Total		120.00	120.00

Narrative: being to record an irrecoverable debt write off in the nominal ledger

General ledger references

The journal must balance

Entering opening balances

In the assessment you may be required to prepare a journal to record opening balances in a new set of accounts.

- The asset balances are entered as debits.
- The liability balances are entered as credits.
- The capital balance is entered as a credit.

Assessment Focus Point: In your assessment the journal entry you are required to prepare will not include narrative but may look like this:

Account name	Amount £	Debit ✓	Credit ✓

Select from picklist   Figure here   Ticks as appropriate

Principles

In an assessment, you will be given wages summaries from which to prepare journal entries.

The total payroll cost is the employees' gross pay plus employer's national insurance contributions (NIC), plus, where applicable, employer's pension contributions:

- Income tax and employees' NIC must be deducted from an employee's gross pay.
- Voluntary deductions may also be made (eg employee pension contributions, trade union fees and give-as-you-earn (GAYE)).

Assessment Focus Point: Essentially you will be asked to complete some of the double entry for the payroll transactions for a business which uses a wages control account.

Example

The following wages summary relates to the month of March 20XX.

Wages summary

	£
Gross wages	17,200
Employer's NIC	2,000
Employee's NIC	1,640
Trade Union fees	280
Income Tax	3,000

Make the relevant entries to record:

(1) The wages expense
(2) The amounts owed to HMRC
(3) Net wages paid to employees
(4) The amounts owed to the Trade Union

Wages expense

(1) Wages control (17,200 + 2,000)	19,200		

Wages control

(2) HMRC (2,000 + 1,640 + 3,000)	6,640	(1) Wages expense	19,200
(3) Trade Union	280		
(4) Bank	12,280		
	19,200		19,200

HMRC

		(2) Wages control	6,640

Trade union

		(3) Wages control	280

Bank

		(4) Wages control (17,200 − 1,640 − 280 − 3,000)	12,280

6: Errors and the trial balance

In an ideal world, all transactions would be entered into the accounts correctly. However because people do make mistakes, a number of checks are carried out to bring these to light. Corrections are then made. Where a mistake caused the two columns of the trial balance to total to different amounts, the correction will involve a suspense account.

Types of error not causing an imbalance on the trial balance

The main types of error are

- **Error of original entry**, eg both entries in the general ledger show £1,000 instead of £10,000

- **Error of reversal of entries**, eg the correct amounts are entered but the debit is shown as the credit and the credit as a debit

- **Error of omission**, eg receive supplier's invoice for £500 and do not record it in the books at all

- **Error of principle**, eg treating capital expenditure as revenue expenditure

- **Error of commission**, eg putting telephone expenses of £250 in the electricity expense account

- **Compensating errors**, eg both sales day book and purchases day book coincidentally miscast by £500

The main types of error are

- **Single entry transactions**, eg only one side of the double entry made to the general ledger

- **Unequal amounts error**, eg one side is entered correctly with £435, but other side is entered incorrectly with £335

- **Two debits/two credits error**, eg both accounts in the general ledger have been entered with debit or both with credit entries

- **Transposition error**, eg writing £381 as £318 (the difference is always divisible by 9) – not always a source of imbalance on the trial balance, if the same transposition error is made in both debit and credit entries

- **Calculation error**, eg a general ledger account has been added up incorrectly

- **Balance omission**, eg a balance on the general ledger has been omitted from the trial balance

- **Balance transfer error**, eg correct balance of £140 in general ledger account is transferred to trial balance as £1,400

Imbalance on TB – practical methods for identifying errors

1. Check the totalling of the debit column and the credit column on the trial balance.
2. Calculate the difference between the debit and credit total. —————

   This may help to spot the difference immediately

3. Check that each balance in the general ledger has been correctly copied into the trial balance and included on the correct side, debit or credit.
4. Check that all the balances in the general ledger have been included in the trial balance.
5. Check that the calculation of the balance on each ledger account is correct.

   Has it been included on the wrong side?

6. Look in the ledger accounts for any entry that is for the same amount as the difference on the trial balance.

   Has it been omitted?

7. Look in the ledger accounts for any entry that is for half the amount of the difference on the trial balance.

   Last resort

8. Check all of the bookkeeping entries from the books of prime entry since the date of the last trial balance.
9. Check that all the books of prime entry have been written up and totalled correctly.

Correcting errors causing an imbalance on the trial balance

A suspense account is a temporary account that is used in the following circumstances

- A difference occurs in the trial balance caused by the incomplete recording of double entry in respect of one or more transactions.
- The difference is entered in a suspense account so the trial balance still balances.

Any balance on a suspense account must be eliminated with correcting journals:

Step 1. Identify incorrect entries that created the suspense account

Step 2. Reverse incorrect entries, clearing the suspense account

Step 3. Make correct entries

Example

Harry Perkins, sole trader, prepared his trial balance for the year ended 30 June 20XX. He found that debits exceeded credits by £7,048.

He has discovered the following errors.

(1) Discounts allowed of £486 were entered to the discounts allowed account as £684 the entry on the SLCA was correctly recorded of £486.
(2) Credit sales totalling £7,500 had not been entered in the sales account.
(3) In respect of telephone expenses of £650, the only entry made was in the cash book.

The balance would be cleared by writing up the suspense account as follows.

SUSPENSE ACCOUNT

	£		£
Discounts allowed (1)	198	B/f	7,048
SLCA (2)	7,500	Bank (3)	650
	7,698		7,698

With suspense accounts it is essential to think carefully about double entry.
Provided you work logically there is no reason why you should not get it right.

Explanation behind the journals

		£	£			£	£
(1)	To reverse the original entry:				DEBIT SLCA	7,500	
	DEBIT Suspense	198			CREDIT Sales		7,500
	DEBIT SLCA	486		(3)	To reverse the original entry:		
	CREDIT Discounts allowed		684		DEBIT Bank	650	
					CREDIT Suspense		650
	To make the correcting journal:						
	DEBIT Discounts allowed	486			To make the correcting journal:		
	CREDIT SLCA		486		DEBIT Telephone	650	
					CREDIT Bank		650
(2)	To reverse the original entry:						
	DEBIT Suspense	7,500					
	CREDIT SLCA		7,500				

Assessment Focus Point: You may be asked to record a journal entry to open a suspense account. It is necessary to be able to understand the errors, and to draw up the journals to correct them.